Original title:
Life: Full of Surprises and Unanswered Questions

Copyright © 2025 Creative Arts Management OÜ
All rights reserved.

Author: Jameson Hartfield
ISBN HARDBACK: 978-1-80566-183-2
ISBN PAPERBACK: 978-1-80566-478-9

The Unknown Horizon

In the morning I woke up late,
Pants on my head, isn't that great?
I searched for my keys, they danced away,
Turns out they were in the fridge all day.

Coffee brewed like a magic potion,
Spilled on the floor, a caffeinated ocean.
I laughed at the cat who looked so perplexed,
Wondering why breakfast felt so unhexed.

Outside, the sun wore a silly hat,
I tripped on a garden gnome while chasing a cat.
A squirrel in a tie gave me a wink,
And I questioned my choices over that drink.

When night fell, stars twinkled with cheer,
I pondered the cosmos while cracking a beer.
The unknown horizon calls with a grin,
And I stumble through wonders, like, where have I been?

Inch by Inch

I wake up each day with a quirky plan,
Discovering why socks vanish, I think I can!
A puzzle of matches, who'd thought it could be,
My missing left shoe just fled to the sea.

At breakfast, the toast took a leap off the plate,
I chased it around, calling, 'Hey, don't be late!'
Butter flew by like a superhero bold,
For breakfast adventures, I've struck pure gold.

Midday, I found a new side of the street,
Where cars do cha-chas and people skip a beat.
A llama in sunglasses looked quite a show,
And I couldn't help wondering where should I go?

As day fades away and the moon whirls around,
I ask no questions, just dance to the sound.
Inch by inch, I embrace what's amiss,
With laughter and stories, there's always a twist!

Fragments of Reality

A sock on the ceiling, how did it get there?
The cat gives me looks, like it knows my despair.
I trip on my shoelace, it's tied in a knot,
The cereal's missing—was it me, or the pot?

My phone's in the fridge, it's cold as a fish,
I ponder my choices, oh make a good wish!
An email from Mars, it's spam, what a joke,
I ask all the pillows, but they can't even poke.

The Chaotic Symphony

A trumpet from nowhere, it blares with a grin,
The dog joins the band, has he lost his sense of sin?
Socks dance on the table, they're cutting a rug,
While ants move in rhythm, they tango and shrug.

I brew a cup of chaos, it spills on my shoe,
The clock's lost its hands, what time could it skew?
A parade of odd creatures, what fun, what delight,
While shares of my sanity dwindle with night.

A Jigsaw of Wonder

Puzzled by puzzles, what piece goes where?
A cat found a corner, now I'm in despair.
The mirror is laughing, it shows me a clown,
While coffee's demanding, 'You better not frown!'

One sock's an explorer, the other's a spy,
A plant's making plans to escape to the sky.
The fridge sings a tune, a lullaby strange,
I smile at the weirdness, embracing the change.

Metamorphosis of Enigma

A frog in a suit, now that's quite a sight,
He dances in circles, he's feeling alright.
The toaster has dreams of being a chef,
While the chair throws a party—quite boldly, I guess!

As socks take a journey, they wander so far,
The remote's on vacation, who knows where they spar?
I trip over questions, a tumble, a fall,
Here's hoping tomorrow brings answers for all.

Glistening Uncertainties

When socks lose their pairs, oh what a plight,
In depths of the dryer, they vanish from sight.
Cups ask for tea, but spill out the grace,
How do they conspire, this curious race?

Jellybeans dance, on a tabletop stage,
Flavors like mysteries, all wrapped in a cage.
You choose red or green, but what's in between?
A taste of delight, or a prank on the scene?

The Odyssey of Intrigue

A cat on a mission, with a glance so sly,
Plotting the downfall of a wayward fly.
It leaps with great gusto, a champion's fight,
Only to land, in its own tail's plight.

The fridge hums secrets, in a nonchalant tune,
Leftover whispers beneath the full moon.
Is that soup getting old, or a fine wine in jest?
One soup's a disaster, the other was blessed.

Burst of Curiosity

A squirrel on a wire, with acorn in tow,
Dreams of skydiving, what a daring show!
Yet, gravity giggles, throws him for a spin,
He ponders the fall, might just take it on a whim.

The remote goes missing, it's a well-known crime,
It hides in the cushions, just biding its time.
Each click-tock of buttons, a path full of twists,
It's an adventure to find it, none can resist!

The Tapestry of the Unseen

A bee in the flowers, holds secrets untold,
What quests does it venture, what dreams does it fold?
Is honey a treasure, or more like a tease?
The buzz of its laughter echoes through leaves.

A sock puppet speaks of the sky and the ground,
Telling tall tales of the sights it has found.
With googly eyes wide, and a mouth full of cheer,
It asks all the questions, but still shows no fear.

Secrets Beneath the Stars

Beneath the vast, twinkling dome,
We wonder if penguins have a home.
Do aliens laugh while they float in space?
Or hide their jokes with a funny face?

Turtles tweet when the moon's on high,
And squirrels debate on why squirrels fly.
We ponder the mysteries of cheese on toast,
As fish hold meetings of what they love most.

The Weight of Wonder

Bags packed full of curiosity,
Got questions that defy gravity.
Why do socks vanish in the wash?
And why do dads always hide the squash?

Kittens plot with stars in their eyes,
While wise old owls share puzzling lies.
Paper boats sail on streams of doubt,
Leaving us giggling, "What's that about?"

A Cup Overflowing

A cup of thoughts that never stay,
Why does toast always fall buttered, I say?
Do pancakes dance on syrupy nights?
As marshmallows whisper of feathered flights?

Cupcakes chuckle, frosting on high,
While gummy bears plot to reach the sky.
A smoothie of dreams that churns and spills,
Leaving behind a trail of thrills.

The Missing Puzzle Piece

Searching for pieces in a wild, jumbled mess,
Wondering why puzzles cause such stress.
Where did that piece with a dragon go?
Maybe it's off to join the show!

Jigsaw cats snicker, their tails all askew,
While wise old raccoons claim they once flew.
Problems stuck like glue, can't make sense,
But laughter's the key, as we jump the fence!

The Mirage of Certainty

I planned my day with great precision,
But found a bird had stole my vision.
My coffee spilled, my toast did fly,
As I chased a squirrel, oh my, oh my!

The map I drew led to a park,
Yet ended up near a giant shark.
With every step, a twist and turn,
I learned the world loves to make us yearn.

A Symphony of Surprises

A doorbell rings, what could it be?
A package, a friend, or just a bee?
The cake I baked, it sank like lead,
Next time I'll stick to toast instead!

My cat decided to join the fray,
Chasing shadows all day, hooray!
Each note a laugh, each pause a jest,
In a world where we jest, we are truly blessed.

Overture of the Unknown

A trip to the store, I lost my way,
Found a rubber chicken, bright and gay.
With every aisle, a brand new quest,
Which cereal will make me feel the best?

The check-out line, a chat with fate,
A guy with a hat that's way too great.
I left with snacks and a smile so wide,
Who knew adventures were right inside?

Moments That Shift

A riddle came from down the street,
A man in socks and flippers on feet.
He asked my name, I told it twice,
Then tripped and fell, oh isn't that nice?

The flowers danced in the summer breeze,
While I pondered life with a face full of cheese.
In every stumble and unexpected pause,
Lies the humor that makes us all applause.

A Whisper of Possibilities

In a world where cows might fly,
And pizza grows on trees up high.
The grass might sing, the rocks might chat,
You never know where the cat's at!

A river flows with soda pop,
And ice cream mountains, oh, they never stop!
When socks go missing, it's quite a scene,
Did they join a circus, or just daydream?

Glimmers of the Unanswered

Why do ducks march in a row?
And where do all our lost shoes go?
Do stars hold secrets in their twinkling light,
Or just enjoy the cozy night?

If toast lands butter-side down,
Is that why we wear a frown?
Could it be that socks conspire,
To vanish when the laundry's dire?

The Dance of Doubt

Oh, who invented the rubber band?
And why do we find it so grand?
Why do monkeys throw their food?
Do they know it sets the mood?

When ice spins in the summer sun,
Is it hiding, just having fun?
Do jellybeans dance when we're not near,
Or do they just pop out of sheer cheer?

Kaleidoscope of Questions

Can fish ride bikes or paint with glee?
What's the point of a bumblebee?
Does chicken really taste like the shoe,
Or is that just a rumor we grew?

If clouds wear hats, do they get cold?
What stories does a pencil hold?
Do ants have parties when we're away,
Or just chill out, surf the day?

Moments of Wonder

A cat sat on a hat with flair,
Its owner gasped, 'How did you dare?'
A bird flew by on a skateboard ride,
While fish took selfies, eyes wide with pride.

The toast popped up with a little dance,
It twirled and flipped, took a wobbly chance.
Then socks ran off with dinner rolls,
In a world where laughter tickles our souls.

The Enigma of Tomorrow

A penguin in shades decorates the night,
Riding a unicycle, oh what a sight!
The sun sings softly to dreaming trees,
While squirrels debate the meaning of cheese.

Time flies past on a pogo stick,
Juggling clocks, oh isn't that slick?
Tomorrow's just a riddle in disguise,
Or maybe a pie in the face of surprise.

Fragments of the Unexplained

Why does the moon wear a silly grin?
As cricket teams compete with violins.
An octopus dines on pizza and fries,
While fish argue 'bout who's wearing the ties.

A ghost rides bikes with a toothy grin,
Playing hopscotch with a cheeky kin.
The clock strikes twelve; confetti rains down,
As dreams frolic in a whimsical town.

Chasing Elusive Dreams

A rabbit in slippers jumps through the air,
In search of sweet carrots; where are they rare?
Chasing whispers of wishes in clouds,
Drifting through giggles and playful crowds.

The donut truck sings a tune offbeat,
While jellybeans dance on their tiny feet.
And as night falls, the stars hold their breath,
Awaiting the jokes that dance after death.

The Serendipity of Moments

A pigeon stole my sandwich fast,
I thought it would be mine to eat.
Instead, I watched my lunch fly past,
While it took off with such a feat.

I tripped on a crack in the street,
But landed where flowers bloom.
I laughed as my foot took the lead,
And suddenly bright was my gloom.

A cat in a hat danced on my fence,
I chuckled, didn't know why.
Is that odd? It makes perfect sense,
When you see the world with a sigh.

Chasing rainbows on Tuesday nights,
With socks that surely don't match.
I bumped into joy, quite by rights,
And found that I had a good catch.

Beyond the Known

A squirrel with shades crossed my path,
I pondered why he dressed so neat.
He offered me snacks, which made me laugh,
But only if I joined the beat.

With question marks in my cereal bowl,
I wondered if it's all a game.
Do fish ponder the depths of a shoal,
Or do they swim without shame?

I spotted a shoe on the lawn,
And thought, 'Well, isn't that poetic?'
Did someone dance, only to yawn?
Perhaps the world is magnetic!

A dog in a cape flew by my side,
He barked like a trumpet, so cute.
As we soared through the nonsensical tide,
I mused, "Is this a dream? Or my commute?"

Threads of Curiosity

Tickling my toes with fuzzy socks,
Unexpected delight in the churn.
I found a pair of mismatched clocks,
That told me time was a twisty turn.

The jellybeans in my pocket jived,
To a rhythm only we could hear.
Did candies become alive and thrive?
Or was it just a sugar-fueled cheer?

Chasing shadows of dancing chairs,
I giggled as they twirled in lines.
Did objects have feelings and cares?
Or were they just bored with the signs?

With a hiccup from the toaster, I sighed,
It spat out toast that clearly had flair.
Why does breakfast always play hide?
In this kitchen of giggles and air!

A Flicker in the Fog

A foghorn whispered a secret joke,
As I tripped over a lengthy riddle.
A fish with a top hat said, 'Don't choke!'
I laughed at the thought of a fiddle.

Through swirling mist, a clue did wait,
A sock went dancing, without a care.
I thought, what a quirky fate,
For a sock to pause and stare!

Streetlamps winked like they knew the score,
As shadows jived on cobbled stones.
What fun could be behind each door?
Perhaps a wall of talking phones!

With giggles hiding in every twist,
And whispers of tomorrow's surprise,
I danced to the songs of the mist,
And smiled at the world's crazy lies.

The Ever-Mutable Canvas

Brushes dance in vibrant hues,
Each stroke a giggle, each shade a muse.
A canvas changes, wild and free,
What's hidden here? Just wait and see!

Colors clash in a silly fight,
A cat on canvas, oh what a sight!
Paint splatters like confetti rain,
Will it be chaos or art? Who's to gain?

Squiggles turn to faces bright,
Monsters lurk in shadows tight.
Yet with each laugh, we paint anew,
The brush is nimble, the world askew.

Whimsy reigns, a sparkling mess,
In colors bold, we find our jest.
Life's vibrant palette, ever askew,
An artist's heart knows just what to do!

Whims of Time

Tick-tock, tick-tock, what a riddle,
Time plays the flute and we dance the middle.
It runs amok, a playful sprite,
Crawls like a snail or takes rapid flight.

Yesterday's toast is today's jam,
Tomorrow's dreams fit in a flimsy pan.
I asked the clock, "Are you my friend?"
It just laughed, "I seldom pretend."

Moments linger like half-baked pies,
Some rise and shine, while others capsize.
A wink from fate, a twist we share,
In the whimsical whirl, we lose our care.

So here's to time, that slippery beast,
With a grin so wide, it'll never cease.
Each tick may tease or bring delight,
In the whims of hours, we find our flight.

On the Edge of a Question

Why do ducks quack with such glee?
What's hidden in that shimmery sea?
Every wonder wears a quirky hat,
Feathered friends chuckle, and we tip our mat.

Is cheese a shape or just a taste?
Or is that thought a silly waste?
Questions dance like leaves in the breeze,
They twirl and spin, trying to tease.

At the tip of curiosity's tongue,
Silly questions make us feel young.
What's so amusing? We can't quite cuff,
But it's the mystery that makes it tough!

Floating thoughts, all jumbled and jive,
In this mind game, we feel alive.
So ask away, let whims collide,
For on the edge, true fun will reside.

Unraveled Mysteries

In the attic lies a dusty box,
Full of secrets, weird paradox.
What's inside? A shoe? A hat?
Or is it just a worn-out spat?

Clocks that tick, but never chime,
Searching for answers takes some time.
Peeking through the curtain's seam,
Finding laughter in every scheme.

A sandwich sings a lullaby,
While socks enact a wobbly spy.
The fridge buzzes with chatter and cheer,
Unraveled mysteries, drawing near!

So let's embrace the quirky clues,
In life's great jigsaw, we can choose.
To laugh, to ponder, to simply jest,
In every question, we find a fest!

Puzzles in the Twilight

In the twilight's dance, shadows play,
Lost socks in the dryer lead us astray.
The clock ticks backward, what a delight,
Is that my dinner or a cat in flight?

Questions bubble up like soda can fizz,
Why do we park our cars in a quiz?
Is it cheese or a hat on my head?
The mystery now keeps me well-fed.

As I ponder why ducks always quack,
I stumble on answers that never look back.
Each bump on the road sends me to jest,
How curious this maze, I must confess!

With riddles lurking in garden weeds,
I ask if a tomato really needs seeds?
Why do phones chirp when no one's around?
Perhaps I'll just dance with the lost and found.

Tales of Uncertainty

In a world of maybes, I flip a coin,
A cat in a hat sings a tune to join.
Should I jump or should I sit?
Every decision feels like a skit.

Rainbows squeeze through the clouds of doubt,
As I search for the route my socks snuck out.
A wild guess here, a wild guess there,
Maybe my shoes have an escape affair.

In this tale, the comma's a pause,
Why do we park in lots without laws?
The ducks waddle on, with their own command,
While I just try to understand their plan.

Night falls softly, a giggle arises,
What's real or imagined? Now that's a surprise!
But I wear a smile, through it all I sway,
Collecting odd stories that brighten my day.

Beneath the Surface

Beneath the layers, a pickle lies,
With questions as crooked as my friend's ties.
Why do doughnuts have holes in their core?
Is there wisdom behind such folklore?

A fish in a suit serves tea with a grin,
What's under the surface? Where do I begin?
Maybe a worm wears a shiny new coat,
Sipping on puddles as if on a boat.

Pillows hold whispers of dreams without end,
Why does the toaster steal bread from a friend?
Each thought tumbles out like a quirky spree,
In this wobbly world, it's just you and me!

The dance of the shadows begins to revive,
Each question a spark keeps our giggles alive.
Under the surface, we dive in delight,
Chasing the wonder throughout every night.

The Garden of What-Ifs

In a garden of wonders, seeds start to sprout,
What if rain's just the sky having doubts?
The bees hold a pollination affair,
Planning their dreams in the fragrant air.

If carrots wear coats, do they know they're root?
What if hedgehogs refuse to play cute?
Every flower's whisper, a tickle of chance,
Windswept confetti leads us to dance.

With each step, questions blossom and twirl,
In this silly garden, let's give it a whirl.
If snails had a race, who would take home gold?
Maybe they'd laugh, their secrets retold.

Oh, the what-ifs, like butterflies roam,
Tickling the petals we call our own home.
So let's chuckle together, embrace the jest,
In this garden of giggles, we're truly blessed.

Questions in the Quiet

In the still night, a cat passed by,
Are they plotting, should I ask why?
The stars giggle in twinkling light,
Maybe they have secrets just out of sight.

The fridge hums a peculiar tune,
Does it hold memories of a spoon?
As I ponder the oddness within,
Does the yogurt dream of cheese and sin?

A sock slipped away, where could it go?
Lost in the realms of laundry woe.
Does it dance happily, or just hide?
Questions fly like birds, oh what a ride!

Tick tock goes the clock on my wall,
Does it laugh at me, or just stall?
Maybe it knows who'll win the race,
The future's a puzzle, a curious case.

The Curious Path Ahead

As I walk on this winding street,
What's that smell? Oh, something sweet!
A duck with a hat gives me a wink,
Does it know more than I think?

A squirrel in shades crosses my way,
Is he on a mission, what does he say?
The trees whisper secrets to the breeze,
Do they gossip like old friends with ease?

A newspaper flies with a headline bright,
'Why did the chicken cross the light?'
Do chickens have answers? Should I inquire?
Or would they fluster, and just retire?

Road signs twist, their arrows spin,
Where will I go, will I just grin?
The path ahead is filled with fun,
What will I find? Oh, let's just run!

Unexpected Twists

A candy wrapper fell on the floor,
Does it hold tales of sweets and more?
The table dances, or was it me?
What secrets does furniture see?

The kettle whistles a high-pitched song,
Is it a melody, or just wrong?
I pour the water, but what's the score?
Is my tea a plot? I want more lore!

The chair creaks like it knows a joke,
Does it understand all that I spoke?
Perhaps it chuckles, in creaks and groans,
At all my questions, and countless moans.

Suddenly, a fly buzzes on by,
With purpose, is it aiming for the sky?
Each little twist makes me stop and stare,
Is a simple moment magic, rare?

Echoes of the Unseen

A shadow leaps behind the door,
Why is it there? What's it looking for?
I chase it down, but it's too sly,
Does it chuckle as it flits by?

Footsteps dance in empty halls,
Are they waiting for someone to call?
Does the floor groan in playful jest,
As it holds the memories of many a guest?

The wind whispers through the trees,
Does it carry tales of ancient bees?
Perhaps it knows where the lost socks hide,
Or the fate of the cats that swiftly glide.

In echoes soft, the unheard sings,
What mysteries does the silence bring?
In the chase of shadows, giggles distract,
Is the unseen world making contact?

Secrets Dance in the Dark

Whispers and giggles swirl around,
In shadows, where odd things abound.
A sock goes missing, what a fright!
It's just the ghost of laundry night.

Ovens hum tunes of food yet to bake,
And spoons argue over who's fake.
The cat holds court on a throne of fluff,
Declaring that life's just silly stuff.

Balloons float by with a cheeky grin,
Inviting us to join in the din.
Who knew surprises could be such a riot?
Oh, the world is indeed a curious diet!

With each tick-tock, there's something new,
Maybe a frog in a bright pink shoe?
So we dance in the glow of the moon,
Chasing waves of giggles, just like a tune.

Vagabonds of Wonder

We wander through fields of cotton candy,
In flip-flops, isn't that just dandy?
The squirrels debate about which tree's best,
While bees throw parties, they never rest.

With pockets full of odd little things,
Like broken hearts or paper rings.
Each twist and turn makes the world seem mad,
But oh, the laughs we often had!

Maps drawn in crayon lead the way,
To treasure chests marked 'Do Not Play'.
Who planted the daisies in a line?
With each petal, we giggle and whine.

So here we roam, vagabonds at heart,
In search of a puzzle, a whimsical art.
With every surprise that we stumble upon,
We toast to the weirdness that carries us on.

The Puzzle of Existence

Jigsaw pieces spill from the box,
Some are cats, and some are rocks.
Why does the corner piece take a stance?
And who taught the weird shapes how to dance?

A pickle and a donut debate on a shelf,
While celery claims it's the fastest of self.
In circles we ponder, scratching our heads,
What meaning is found in toast that just spreads?

The clock's hands are tired from all the fate spins,
Counting the minutes as laughter begins.
Each tick reveals questions that bubble and fizz,
Like soda pop thoughts, what is this whizz?

So let's solve this riddle, however absurd,
One giggle at a time, not a sound heard.
For hidden in laughter, beyond every tear,
We find bits of answers, wrapped up in cheer.

Between What Was and What Could Be

Between yesterday's cake and tomorrow's pie,
We stumble through moments on the fly.
Toys left in corners whisper and sigh,
As socks chase dust bunnies fluttering by.

A frog with a monocle sips from a cup,
Declaring the day we should all liven up!
Each twist in the road hides secrets and jokes,
Where shadows uncover absurd little folks.

The sun winks and giggles, playing its game,
Reminding us all that we're never the same.
With each passing glance, a new tale takes flight,
Between what we've seen and what feels just right.

So let's skip through the gaps with a skip and a hop,
Dance in the echoes, let laughter not stop.
For here, in the spaces where odd things agree,
We find the best moments, wild and carefree.

The Unwritten Chapters

The pen is poised, but where to write?
A cake of chaos gleams so bright.
Each turn of page, a riddle to face,
Do I start with a dance or a graceful chase?

The coffee spills, oh what a scene,
A plot twist hidden in the caffeine.
Characters stumble, trip, then fall,
Do they get up? Who can recall?

The twist of fate makes us grin,
Laundry's lost socks, where have they been?
A chapter opens, and then it's gone,
Was it a dream, or just a con?

So write it down, or let it fade,
An empty page, a fun charade.
With laughter echoing through the space,
We find the fun in every trace.

Whispers in the Wind

A gusty breeze with jokes to share,
It tickles my ear, light as air.
What were the words that danced in glee?
Just fleeting whispers teasing me.

The trees all chuckle, the birds all jest,
Nature giggles, it's doing its best.
Here's a riddle tossed in flight,
Where does the sun go after night?

Clouds are busy knitting dreams,
With yarn of sunlight, or so it seems.
Oh, the wind carries tales so bold,
Of secrets hidden and stories told.

So if you listen, with heart so light,
You may just catch a joke in flight.
For every breeze that bends and sways,
There's laughter lurking in the ways.

The Unfolding Map

A map unrolled, oh where to go?
With paths that wander, we take it slow.
Treasure marks and X's draw,
But what's a shortcut? I forget the law.

My compass spins, what's north or south?
A quick detour? Just figure it out!
Tangled routes with twists and turns,
For every misstep, my wanderlust burns.

Each stop a giggle, each turn a tease,
Found a taco stand by the trees.
With every fork, my stomach grins,
Wherever we roam, that's where fun begins.

So let's embrace this winding way,
With maps that don't quite want to play.
Adventure waits, with questions anew,
As we draw our path, it's all up to you.

Shadows of Tomorrow

In twilight hours, shadows dance,
What do they whisper? Take a chance.
They stretch and sway in funny ways,
Do they giggle? Oh, what a craze!

Each silhouette holds stories tall,
Who knew a shadow could start a brawl?
With laughter echoing through the night,
A game of hide-and-seek, pure delight.

Flickering lights play hide and seek,
While uncertainty dances, oh so sleek.
What's waiting just beyond that door?
Is it fortune, or a big ol' bore?

So lean in close, and take a peek,
Tomorrow's secrets, they love to sneak.
With every step, let laughter flow,
As we chase those shadows, to and fro.

In Praise of the Unpredictable

A squirrel with sunglasses, in the trees,
Wearing a hat, just to tease.
Who knew breakfast could fly so high?
Pancakes? Or did I just sigh?

A twist in the plot, oh what a scene,
Lost my keys where my cat's been.
What's next, a dance-off with a chair?
Up is down, and it's quite the affair!

Lemons turn sweet on a whim,
And your sock drawer could make you grin.
Rabbits in top hats steal the show,
Let's spin this world, go with the flow!

Oh, flip a coin, see where it lands,
Should I buy ice cream or join a band?
Each choice, a giggle or a gasp,
In the unexpected, we find our clasp.

The Song of What-If

What if cats wore shoes, oh what a sight!
Would they prance or take flight?
Imagining muffins that talk back,
And a dog that can roller skate down the track.

What if trees could laugh at my jokes?
Would they drop acorns or simply poke?
Shall we dance in the rain with a hat?
Or chase a raccoon while we're at that?

What if the moon were made of cheese?
I'd sail my ship through a snack attack, if you please!
Balloons that whisper secrets to bees,
And chocolate rivers flowing with ease.

With each "what if," a giggle appears,
Laughter rings loud, no need for fears.
Embrace the strange, let your mind roam,
In a world of wonders, we make our home!

A Flicker of Possibility

A light bulb flickers, what a tease,
Should I fix it? Or let it freeze?
Maybe a dance to the buzzing beat,
Or invite the shadows for a treat!

A fortune cookie in hand, cracked wide,
Should I trust a slip from the inside?
"You'll meet someone at the zoo!" it boasts,
But I just go to see the ghostly hosts.

What if the pancakes were made of gold?
Or the dog knew tales of brave and bold?
Each moment's a twist, a little surprise,
Life's best kept secrets are in disguise.

So let's light up candles, dance in the dark,
Each flicker a chance for a lark.
No map for the roads that we dare take,
Just laughter and grit, and a promise to wake!

Chasing the Unfathomable

Chasing rainbows, both near and far,
Could I catch one in a jar?
A fish in boots, would it chase me too?
What's it pondering in its slippery stew?

The toaster's a wizard in morning light,
Sometimes it burns, a dramatic fight!
Should I cheer for the toast with a smile,
Or give it a break, just for a while?

An octopus knitting in the bay,
Who knew crafting could be so cliché?
Dreams unravel in colors so bright,
As we chase the unfathomable, holding on tight.

With giggles and quirks, let's run wild,
Every moment's a treasure, just like a child.
So bring your oddities, your silly delight,
In the chase of the unknown, we find the right!

A Tapestry of Queries

Why do socks vanish in the wash?
Are gnomes dancing on the lawn?
Why is cereal a soup, oh my?
And where's the remote I've withdrawn?

Cats plotting world domination schemes,
While we search for that odd shoe.
Is the toast always burnt on one side?
Or do fairies just like to undo?

Why do we trip over our own feet?
Yet glide when we've had too much wine?
It's the curious quirks of our days,
That keep us laughing quite fine!

And what's that noise at midnight's toll?
A ghost? A raccoon rummaging near?
With riddles wrapped tight in the night,
We dance with confusion and cheer!

Stardust and Questions

Why does every shoe squeak on floors?
Is it a signal from outer space?
Why do we laugh till our sides ache?
While our reflection wears a puzzled face?

Do ants hold conferences on crumbs?
Plotting a course like tiny spies?
Is the moon really made of cheese?
Or just a giant light in disguise?

Why does the toaster burn my bread?
A conspiracy from kitchenware?
And why do we only lose our keys
When we're already late, I declare!

At every corner, questions bloom,
With stars twinkling in the dark.
We're just curious cosmic jesters,
In a universe that leaves its mark!

The Journey Beyond Knowing

Why do we ponder the infinite?
While balancing spoons on our nose?
Do clouds ever question their shape?
Or do they just float where wind blows?

How come cake tastes better with friends?
Is ice cream just frozen delight?
When do we find that missing sock?
On a quest in the depth of night?

Why do plants sway in the breeze?
Are they dancing to a hidden tune?
Questions sprout like weeds in spring,
With answers hidden beyond the moon!

Am I talking to you or to me?
In reflections of laughter and cheer?
We traverse this journey unclear,
With giggles echoing far and near!

Fleeting Glimmers

What's with the cat in the garden?
Is she plotting a zoo escape?
And why do birds sound like they're joking?
Is their chatter just silly drape?

Do fish in bowls hold debates?
Over the best way to swim by?
Why does popcorn jump in the pot?
Is it trying to reach for the sky?

Do you ever forget what you said?
Like a squirrel lost in a chase?
Or is it just part of the fun?
These quirks we wear, a gilded face!

Every moment, a riddle anew,
With laughter weaving through the doubt.
In this kaleidoscope of questions,
We find joy in what life's about!

Horizons of Mystery

In the morning, coffee spills,
Juggling thoughts like clownish thrills.
Socks that vanish in the wash,
Is it magic? What a posh!

The cat meows with utmost grace,
As if demanding a warm embrace.
Where have all my keys now hid?
I guess in the pockets of the kid!

Strange things lurk in every bend,
Like that old college friend named Sven.
With tales so wild, a laugh or two,
Are they true? We may never rue!

Yet through the quirks and surprise,
We find joy beneath the skies.
With wonder in our daily quest,
Who knew not knowing was the best?

The Open-Ended Story

Once I met a dancing spoon,
Who sang me songs beneath the moon.
A story starts without a map,
Oh, what fun to take a nap!

Plot twists come like squirrels on trees,
Biting at your toes with ease.
Where it goes? Well, who can say?
Tomorrow brings a brand new play!

And every chapter, bold or weak,
Leaves us longing for the peak.
The pen's uncapped, and off we fly,
Making sense? Oh, a sweet lie!

So here's to all the tales we weave,
With mystery that we believe.
Let's laugh together, come what may,
In this grand story, we all play!

Dancing with the Unexpected

In a tutu made of socks,
I twirl and leap past silly clocks.
Oh, what a waltz with purple shoes,
Tick-tock surprises, which should I choose?

The oven dings, but what's inside?
A cake, a pie, or just some pride?
A recipe lost, but joy remains,
With laughter dancing through the chains.

Three unexpected guests arrive,
With stories that make laughter thrive.
We juggle cakes, we twirl our tales,
As popcorn flies and humor sails!

So let's embrace the random night,
With every twist, our hearts take flight.
For in the odd, we find delight,
Dancing through life's playful light!

Threads of Hope and Wonder

A knot appeared in my shoelace,
As if it needed its own space.
Yet when I tripped, I just laughed,
For silly slips can be quite daft!

A button popped off my coat,
Floating away like a tiny boat.
What stories could that button tell?
Floating freely, wishing well!

Each thread we weave tells us to hope,
In tangled yarns, we learn to cope.
With every loop, a strange delight,
More crazy patterns come to light!

So gather round, let's stitch and sing,
With laughter that brightens everything.
For in the odd, we find our way,
Woven tightly, come what may!

When Dreams Collide

In a world of mixed-up wishes,
A cat plays poker with a fish.
The sky rains chocolate every night,
While dogs ride bikes, oh what a sight!

A sandwich talks, with cheese and ham,
Debating why a dog says 'wham!'
The stars align, but can't agree,
Is the moon a cow or a giant pea?

Flying toasters toast their bread,
While one claims it can dance instead.
Coffee spills while tea is steeped,
And all the secrets that we've kept!

Oh, what a circus, what a show,
When dreams collide with nowhere to go!
A rubber duck wrestles with fate,
And life's just a quirky first date!

The Silent Compass

A compass spun without a sound,
Pointing north, but feeling down.
It yearns for cheese, and maybe bread,
As maps grow legs and run instead!

An octopus wears a pointy hat,
While plotting how to spoon a cat.
With whispers soft as autumn leaves,
The compass laughs, 'Through webs, who weaves?'

Socks debate the perks of shoes,
While a clock sings out the evening news.
Sticky notes are stuck in fight,
On trivia: who sleeps better at night?

Silent whispers, what a mess,
Where each turn leads to happiness.
In this dance of wild delight,
The compass grins and twirls in flight!

Wandering Hearts and Minds

Hearts that skip like stones on lakes,
Minds that chatter, for goodness' sakes!
A butterfly asks, 'What's the plot?'
While shoes wander, but shoes are not!

A squirrel recites a brand-new rhyme,
About lost socks, oh fun and prime.
The echo laughs, 'Can you find me?'
While a bee buzzes, 'Not a decree!'

Floating bubbles join in the game,
Confetti falls, but it's all the same.
In a parade of silly sights,
Time plays hide and seek at nights!

Wandering hearts get tangled near,
In this glorious, unexpected cheer.
Mind the gap, or maybe soar,
As hearts and minds ask for more!

Encounters Uncharted

A pickle danced with a gray raccoon,
Under a bright and smiling moon.
It whispered secrets to a shoe,
And asked, 'What's odd? A duck or two?'

Stars collided in a fit of giggles,
While jellybeans did silly wiggles.
A teapot rode a speedboat fast,
Querying, 'Will this moment last?'

Kites tangled into playful knots,
While ice cream licked the sun, a lot!
Croissants chatted with loud trumpets,
Debating colors with wild puppets!

This mapless trip, let's never end,
As uncharted dreams weave and bend.
With every turn, the laughter sings,
In bizarre worlds where joy takes wing!

Treasures in the Shadows

In corners we find things so rare,
A sock with a hole, a lost teddy bear,
The cat's secret stash, a pile of fluff,
Life's little treasures can be quite tough.

A treasure map drawn in crayon bright,
Leads to the couch on a lazy night,
Mistaken beliefs of gold-dusted dreams,
Turned out to be crumbs, or so it seems.

We laugh at the finds in the oddest places,
A cookbook mix-up with alien faces,
The cookies that burned, still bring us cheer,
A reminder that chaos is always near.

With surprises that make us chuckle and grin,
Unraveling puzzles we never begin,
In shadows, we dance, with a wink and a smile,
Celebrating moments that last for a while.

The Geometry of Questions

Why is a circle round, and not a square?
Are fish just swimmers, or do they really care?
We ponder the angles of silly debates,
While dodging perplexities thrown by our mates.

Triangles whisper secrets we can't understand,
Angles that dance, like a marching band,
Is a potato a vegetable or a root?
We measure confusion wearing a big boot.

With laughter we calculate how to cope,
As an octagon tries to sell us some hope,
Life's little riddles patched together with glee,
Leaving us wondering, "What could it be?"

Connecting the dots, we lose all our pride,
For in these odd shapes, we can't seem to hide,
Flowing with questions, we giggle and sway,
Finding the fun in the baffling way.

Snippets of the Unexpected

A knock at the door from a pizza in spring,
"Not a delivery!" makes the doorbell ring,
With toppings of laughter and crusts made of fun,
We slice up our worries 'til day is done.

Umbrellas appear when the sun is in sight,
Rainbow sprinkles fall from the clouds in delight,
With each twist of fate, we waddle and spin,
The juice from the lemons makes us grin.

A sock puppet speaks of a long-ago tale,
While jellybeans plot a grand treasure trail,
Popcorn explosions grace our evenings together,
As whispers of friendship float light as a feather.

In snippets we find the joy of surprise,
Unexpected delights are all around us, guys,
Filling our days with giggles and cheer,
In this wondrous ride, let's steer without fear.

Footprints on Clouded Paths

Walking on clouds with shoes made of air,
Finding the way when you're not even there,
With footprints that giggle and laugh on the run,
Every misstep brings sparkles and fun.

We stroll through the mist with our mirrors in hand,
With all of our questions, we form our own band,
Sideways and crooked, yet never alone,
In this jumbled journey, we make it our own.

Rainbows and puddles collide on the ground,
While clouds craft the tales that are happily found,
Every strut and every hop turns the world upside down,
Filling our pockets with laughs and a frown.

In clouded paths, we dance, sing, and play,
Finding drops of magic along the way,
With every adventure causing a spark,
We trace playful paths, wherever we embark.

Lost in the Labyrinth

I wandered through a maze so wide,
With signs that danced and twists that lied.
A squirrel winked, said, "Turn left here!"
But I doubt he meant what he made clear.

Two paths diverged, both looked the same,
One led to cheese, the other, a game.
I took a chance, oh what a sight,
A cheese ball party, my new delight!

But wait! Where's the exit? Where's my phone?
I texted my friends, but they just groaned.
"Quit clowning around and find your way!"
Next time, I'll bring a GPS for play.

In this maze of wonder and merry surprise,
I laughed and tumbled, where foolishness lies.
So here's my tip when paths look absurd:
Just dance with the squirrels, don't take their word!

The Color of Intrigue

In a world where green is not just a shade,
Purple cows prance, their magic displayed.
Orange cats plot in the moonlight's gleam,
Whispering secrets, or so it would seem.

Every morning, a new hue awakes,
A rainbow of choices that twists and shakes.
Should I wear red or maybe sky blue?
Or perhaps it's time for a bright shade of goo?

Then comes a coat that sparkles like stars,
With pockets that giggle and tiny guitars.
"Play me a jingle when life gets too tough!"
I shrugged and agreed, but was that enough?

So through the kaleidoscope, I take a chance,
With every odd color, I twirl and dance.
Life's crazy palette paints questions galore,
But with every shade, I simply want more!

Tides of Fate

The ocean rolled in with a cheeky grin,
As I found a message in a bottle — so thin.
It read, "Beware the crab that wears a crown!"
But I thought, "What's next? A dolphin in a gown?"

The waves took bets on what was to come,
A fish in a tux playing the drum.
While sea turtles shrieked at every new twist,
I felt like a clown on a bubblegum list.

Sailing on dreams, I met a sea star,
Who gave me directions to a steakhouse bazaar.
"Order the splash, it's truly divine!"
But my plate came back with a note and a line.

"Dear diner, your fate's made of foam,
Keep laughing, dear friend – this sea isn't home!"
For the tides rolled out with a merry goodbye,
I waved to the crab, and to my next pie.

When Tomorrow Calls

Tomorrow rang in on a rubbery phone,
Said, "Hey there, buddy, you're not alone!"
I woke up with dreams of grand things to do,
But it offered me waffles... my heart said, "Oh boo!"

"Skip the big plans, let's go for a stroll!"
But tomorrow just giggled, "You need to eat coal?"
With pancakes and syrup, it coaxed and applied,
While I tried to get all my ambition to ride.

So I tossed out my schedule, let futures collide,
With a fork in my hand and a pancake slide.
Tomorrow's a joker, so I'll play along,
Jazz up my routine, sing a silly song!

From point A to point B, if things go akimbo,
I'll laugh at the chaos, and dance to the limbo.
For tomorrow may twist, and run wild with glee,
So I'll take a bite and embrace the folly!

Unfolding Mysteries

A sock goes missing, what a mess,
Invisible creatures, I must confess.
Dinner burns while I sip my tea,
Who knew cooking could be such a spree?

I found my keys inside the fridge,
Was that a dream or a life in a bridge?
Questions swirl like leaves in the wind,
Turns out capers are what I rescind!

I chased a cat, thought it was a clue,
It slipped away, me laughing too.
Mysteries hide beneath my bed,
What's that, a monster or just my shed?

Each twist and turn, like a playful jest,
Unraveling secrets, it's quite the quest.
With giggles and grins, I roam the day,
Who knows what awaits? Let's just play!

The Dance of Shadows

Under the moon, shadows leap and twirl,
Are they friends or foes? Oh what a swirl!
A tap on the window, a trick of the light,
Turns out it's just my cat, with quite the fright!

I lost my sandwich, where could it go?
Did it jump away, or is it a show?
The fridge won't tell me, it keeps its peace,
Guess I'll just snack on the crumbs of my feast!

Unafraid, I strut with a goofy grin,
The shadows are dancing, let's join in!
Laughter echoes into the night,
What a whimsical, silly sight!

Tomorrow holds wonders, I cannot wait,
More fun and games, it's getting late.
I'll take my chances, embrace the weird,
With a wink, I promise not to be feared!

Whispers of the Unknown

In the attic, there's a box of old shoes,
Are they for dancing or just sad blues?
Echoes of laughter soften the air,
Yet no one's here, just dust everywhere!

A rubber chicken squeaks, what a delight,
Is this my new mascot? It surely might!
Questions hang like ghosts on the wall,
Are you all watching me? Come out, stand tall!

I mixed my spices with last night's stew,
Now it tastes like something I never knew.
A dash of humor in every bite,
Who knew dinner could be such a fright?

With giggles and snickers, I dance through the day,
Whispers of secrets lead me astray.
Adventure awaits where laughter bursts,
In the unknown, my heart just thirsts!

Serendipity's Embrace

A trip to the store for some milk and bread,
But I came back with a llama instead!
How did that happen? Who can explain?
Only in dreams do we withstand such gain!

I tripped on my shoelace, fell on the floor,
Found a lost penny, now I'm rich for sure!
What to do next? Perhaps a new dance,
Or play hide and seek, take that chance!

On Monday, I wore socks of mismatch,
Turns out it's fashion! My friends might catch.
Each odd adventure leads to a cheer,
What's next, I wonder, with giggles near!

In this swirling journey of silly things,
I'll embrace the unknown, let joy take wings.
With humor, I strut, through each twisty space,
In the arms of surprise, I find my place!

Windows to the Unexpected

Behind the glass, a squirrel stares,
With acorns piled, he doesn't care.
A bird nearby sings out a tune,
Will it rain or be sunny soon?

A mailbox creaks, a letter flies,
Invitations to strange new highs.
A pizza thief on a bicycle ride,
Takes more than just toppings—but oh, the pride!

The cat plots schemes, with subtle flair,
While old dad naps in the sunny chair.
What's next, a chorus line of frogs?
Will they dance from logs to the morning fogs?

And at dusk, the moon takes a peek,
Who knew a calendar could be so cheek?
A flare for chaos, it kills the calm,
And yet, there's humor, amid the qualm.

The Journey's Riddle

Off on a trip to a place unknown,
With snacks piled high and books overgrown.
The GPS spins in a confused dance,
'Turn left at the taco stand'—what a chance!

A flat tire blooms in the middle of nowhere,
With llamas nearby, it's hardly a scare.
Maps unfold with enticing charms,
Is that a castle, with space for our arms?

A pit stop fills, with quirky finds,
Socks shaped like toast, fun for our minds.
A question looms, should we go or stay?
Strange new paths beckon; come what may!

As shadows stretch under the bright sky,
Magical mysteries float by and sigh.
What's next? A llama in a tux?
Hold tight, dear friends, it's full of luck!

Beneath the Surface

A puddle glimmers, secrets unfurl,
With tiny battles of frog and twirl.
Reflecting patches of sky and dreams,
What happens next? It's wilder than it seems!

Ducks debate their fashion choice,
While turtles come forth to make their voice.
In every ripple, a giggle hides,
Do fish know we're laughing at their slides?

As night descends, stars pop and shine,
What's with that UFO? Is it all a design?
A playful nudge from the great unknown,
With every splash, another whim is shown.

And here we sit, on the brink of night,
With riddles wrapped in delightful fright.
What's under here? We might not know,
With bubbles speaking tales of a colorful show!

A Dance with Uncertainty

In shoes untied, we twirl and glide,
Under the disco ball, what a ride!
Our steps may falter, and that's okay,
A stutter-step here? Just join the play!

A twist of fate, a spin of chance,
With chickens in hats, it's our dance of romance!
Who knew the cat could breakdance too?
We'll follow its lead; let's shimmy right through!

Wobbly waltz with a sandwich in hand,
It spills mustard! Oh, isn't it grand?
Laughter erupts like confetti in air,
With whims of the world, we toss out our care.

And as the night draws to a close,
Questions swirl like leaves in chose.
What was this night? A blur or a plan?
With joy and surprises, we'll dance on, we can!

Echoes of the Unknown

In the morning light, my socks don't match,
A mystery unfolds with every batch.
Is it a style I just don't see?
Or the laundry's joke played on me?

A bird in the sky may drop some news,
But I can't tell if it's good or abuse.
My lunch might be a feast or a spit,
Life's quirky wonders can be quite a hit!

When the phone rings, my heart starts to race,
Is it a message, or just spam's embrace?
I grab it with hope, but it's only my mate,
Who wants to discuss the best pizza rate!

And while dancers twirl beneath the moon,
I'm stuck here pondering if I should swoon.
Each laugh is a puzzle, a riddle to crack,
What tickles the funny bone? I'll take it back.

Paths Not Taken

A fork in the road, my choices abound,
Do I go left for cookies or right for the hound?
Each path is a gamble, a dizzy delight,
Who knew snacks could lead to such a plight?

The elevator broke; I'm stuck on the floor,
Who would've guessed that I'd make a new score?
I chat with a plant; it's got quite a wit,
Turns out it's great company for a bit!

I spotted a squirrel with a glorious stash,
Should I trade it a peanut? Is that too brash?
Each twist in my journey's a wild game of chance,
Perhaps I'll find answers in the squirrel's dance!

When pondering mysteries with friends in tow,
We wonder where socks go when they leave in a row.
The question remains, with laughter it sags,
Are they lost in the void or in pockets of rags?

The Unseen Thread

A spider spins webs of invisible strands,
Could these be the secrets of unknown lands?
Each twist and each turn leads to jest or to scare,
Do the ants have a clue? Do they even care?

Penguins in tuxedos walking the shore,
Are they off to a party or just looking for more?
With every odd sight, my giggle runs free,
Maybe nature's just playing a trick on me!

When rain starts to fall and umbrellas deflate,
I dodge like a ninja, oh man, that was fate!
The puddles are laughing, they splatter and gleam,
But somehow I'm left with a soaked-up regime.

Down the road lies a sign, big and bright,
It points to a place called "Maybe Tonight."
With vague destinations, we wander and blend,
Wherever we're going, let's see where it ends!

Questions at Dusk

The sun dips low, questions swirl and twirl,
Did I leave the stove on or just let it unfurl?
As shadows get longer, and crickets take stage,
I ponder the meaning of this silly age.

Do clouds hold the answers or burps of the sky?
Why do we find joy when we're meant to sigh?
The answers elude, like elusive soap bubbles,
But laughter erupts amidst all of our troubles.

Why's toast always burnt, yet the bread's not so hot?
Is it something in 'fate' or the way I forgot?
With coffee in hand, as the stars start to peek,
The questions keep flowing, but the answers stay weak.

With friends gathered round, we laugh 'til we ache,
In the glow of the dusk, it's a sweet little break.
Perhaps in the fuss, in the joys and the jest,
The answers don't matter; it's the fun we ingest!

The Charm of Chaos

A cat in a tree, oh what a sight,
Chasing its tail, with all of its might.
Laughter erupts, and coffee spills wide,
As chaos unfolds, like a carnival ride.

The toast burns black, the eggs go splat,
The dog wears a hat, imagine that!
With every mistake, we grin and we cheer,
In this wacky dance, there's nothing to fear.

Life takes a twist, like a slide in the park,
With bumps and with curves, just follow the spark.
Each hiccup a joke, a twist of the fate,
Embrace the absurd; it's never too late!

So here's to the mess, the jests on the way,
The charm of the chaos that brightens your day.
We'll giggle and dance, with joy we'll combust,
In this whirlwind of funny, oh yes, we trust!

Embracing the Unexpected

A doorbell rang, it's a llama, uh-oh!
With a bow tie and glasses, stealing the show.
Who ordered this guest? It's quite the surprise,
But laughter erupts, as the chaos complies.

Then a raincloud falls, right onto my head,
With umbrellas in hand, we dance with dread.
The sun peeks through, wearing shades of delight,
A party for puddles, we splash with all might.

A squirrel takes my lunch, oh what a feat!
Stealing my sandwich, then off to retreat.
But the joy in the chase is a treasure untold,
In the wacky mishaps, life's wonders unfold.

So here's to the weird, the silly and fun,
To unexpected chaos, we laugh and we run.
In the playground of fate, let's swing and let be,
With each twist and turn, smiles come naturally!

The Canvas of Dreams

Paint splatters fly, as I pick up a brush,
But who knew a dog would join in the rush?
With colors so bright, it's a whimsical mess,
And laughter erupts, in our playful stress.

Each stroke tells a tale, of odd little things,
Like a chicken in boots or a cat with some wings.
The canvas is wild, full of quirks and delight,
Where questions just dance in the soft morning light.

Yet dreams take a turn, like a kite in the breeze,
With wishes that swirl and tickle the trees.
I paint with my heart, then spill all the paint,
The angels just giggle, as colors grow faint.

With splashes of fun, and wild strokes of fate,
Each canvas a story, let's celebrate!
In the art of the odd, we find heartfelt schemes,
And laugh at the magic within our wild dreams!

Bottled Questions

I found a few questions, bottled like wine,
Curiosities bubbling, they sparkle and shine.
What's that in the sky? Is it a bird or a plane?
Or just my lunch flying, with a sense of disdain?

Why do socks vanish? Where do they go?
Are they off on adventures, putting on a show?
The toaster hides secrets, as it pops and sings,
With mysteries brewing, oh, the joy that it brings!

A pickle walks in, wearing a frown,
"Is a cucumber just a veggie with a crown?"
With fermented giggles, we ponder, we chew,
In this odd little wonder, there's always a clue.

So let's crack those questions, let laughter be known,
In bottles of whimsy, joy seeds are sown.
For each silly thought is a spark in disguise,
And in bottled confusion, true fun never dies!

www.ingramcontent.com/pod-product-compliance
Lightning Source LLC
Chambersburg PA
CBHW072145200426
43209CB00051B/473